THE ELT GRAPHIC NOVEL
William Shakespeare

Script by John McDonald
Adapted for ELT by Brigit Viney

HEINLE
CENGAGE Learning™

Australia • Brazil • Japan • Korea • Mexico • Singapore • Spain • United Kingdom • United States

HEINLE
CENGAGE Learning

Henry V: The ELT Graphic Novel
William Shakespeare
Script by John McDonald
Adapted for ELT by Brigit Viney

Publisher: Bryan Fletcher

Editor in Chief: Clive Bryant

Development Editor: Jennifer Nunan

Content Project Editor: Natalie Griffith

Pencils: Neill Cameron

Inks: Bambos

Colouring: Jason Cardy and Kat Nicholson

Lettering: Nigel Dobbyn

Manufacturing Manager: Helen Mason

Cover / Text Designer: Jo Wheeler

Compositor: Jo Wheeler and
    Parkwood Composition Service, Inc.

Audio: EFS Television Production Ltd.

ISBN: 978-1-4240-2875-7

Heinle
Cheriton House, North Way, Andover, Hampshire, SP10 5BE, UK

Cengage Learning is a leading provider of customized learning solutions with office locations around the globe, including Singapore, the United Kingdom, Australia, Mexico, Brazil and Japan. Locate our local office at: **international.cengage.com/region**

Cengage Learning products are represented in Canada by Nelson Education, Ltd.

Visit Heinle online at **http://elt.heinle.com**
Visit our corporate website at **www.cengage.com**

Published in association with Classical Comics Ltd.

Printed in Italy
2 3 4 5 6 7 8 9 10 - 11 10 09

Contents

Characters

King Henry the Fifth
King of England

Duke Of Gloucester
Brother to the King

Duke Of Bedford
Brother to the King

Duke Of Exeter
Uncle to the King

Duke Of York
Cousin to the King

Earl Of Salisbury

Earl Of Westmoreland

Earl Of Warwick

Archbishop Of Canterbury

Bishop Of Ely

Earl Of Cambridge
Conspirator

Henry, Lord Scroop of Masham
Conspirator

Sir Thomas Grey
Conspirator

Sir Thomas Erpingham
Officer in King Henry's army

Captain Gower
Officer in King Henry's army

Captain Fluellen
Officer in King Henry's army

Captain Macmorris
Officer in King Henry's army

Captain Jamy
Officer in King Henry's army

John Bates
Soldier in King Henry's army

Alexander Court
Soldier in King Henry's army

Characters

Michael Williams
*Soldier in
King Henry's army*

Pistol
*Soldier in
King Henry's army*

Nym
*Soldier in
King Henry's army*

Bardolph
*Soldier in
King Henry's army*

Boy
Servant

A Herald

Charles the Sixth
King of France

Lewis
The Dauphin

Duke Of Bourbon
French Duke

Duke Of Burgundy
French Duke

Duke Of Orleans
French Duke

**The Constable of
France**

Lord Rambures
French Lord

Lord Grandpré
French Lord

Montjoy
French Herald

Queen Isabel
Queen of France

Katherine
*Daughter to
Charles and Isabel*

Alice
*A lady attending on
Katherine*

Hostess of a tavern
*Formerly Mistress
Quickly*

Chorus

Summary

It is the 15th century in England. The **Archbishop** of Canterbury, the head of the Church in England, is worried. The King, Henry the Fifth, might agree to a new law which will take a lot of money and power from the Church. The Archbishop wants to stop him. He tells him he has the right to claim the **throne** of France. Henry writes to Charles the Sixth of France and the **Dauphin,** Charles's son, sends him an unpleasant reply. Henry decides to go to war with France. However he can only take a small **army** because he has to leave some soldiers in England. They are needed to defend the country against the **Scots.**

The French pay three of Henry's **lords** to kill him, but Henry discovers their plan. The three men are **arrested** and killed. Henry goes to France and takes control of the town of Harfleur after a lot of fighting. A lot of his men are killed. Henry wants to take his army home before winter, but the French want to have a big **battle** with him. They want to defeat him and show him their strength. Henry decides to stay and fight.

Before this big battle, Henry puts on ordinary clothes and walks around his camp. He talks to some soldiers and discovers how they feel about the battle and himself. The next day at the Battle of Agincourt, the English army wins, although the French army is much bigger. Henry returns to England.

A few years later, the English and French make peace. The French agree to Henry's demands. Henry will marry **Princess** Katherine of France and will become King of France when Charles the Sixth dies. England and France will be at peace.

ACT One
Scene One

LONDON. A ROOM IN THE KING'S *PALACE*.

SPRING, IN THE YEAR 1415. THE *ARCHBISHOP* OF CANTERBURY AND THE *BISHOP* OF ELY ARE HAVING A CONVERSATION.

THEY'RE TRYING TO PASS THAT LAW AGAIN. WHEN THE LAST KING WAS ALIVE, THEY ALMOST PASSED IT, BUT THEY COULDN'T.

HOW CAN WE STOP IT NOW?

WE MUST THINK ABOUT IT. IF IT IS PASSED, WE'LL LOSE A LOT OF OUR LAND AND PROPERTY.

IT WILL COST US A HUGE AMOUNT OF MONEY!

WE'LL HAVE NOTHING LEFT!

NOTHING AT ALL!

HOW CAN WE STOP IT?

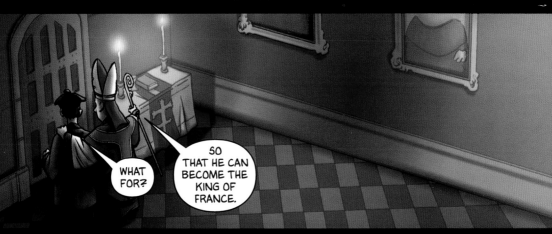

ACT ONE

Scene Two

LONDON. IN THE KING'S *PALACE* — SPRING 1415. KING HENRY V IS MEETING SOME IMPORTANT PEOPLE.

WHERE IS THE *ARCHBISHOP* OF CANTERBURY?

NOT HERE.

PLEASE ASK HIM TO COME HERE.

SHALL WE CALL IN THE *AMBASSADOR*, MY *LORD*?

NOT YET. I WANT TO HEAR ABOUT FRANCE FROM THE ARCHBISHOP.

GOD *BLESS* THE KING!

THANK YOU. PLEASE EXPLAIN HOW I HAVE A CLAIM TO THE FRENCH *THRONE*.

I WANT YOU TO TELL ME THE COMPLETE TRUTH.

A LOT OF MEN COULD DIE IF WE GO TO WAR OVER THIS.

IF WE ARE IN THE WRONG, IT WILL BE YOUR *FAULT*.

SO TELL THE TRUTH. I'M LISTENING.

13

14

HE IS REMINDING ME OF MY WILDER DAYS, WHEN I WAS YOUNGER.

BUT TELL THE *DAUPHIN*: I WILL BE A KING AND SHOW MY TRUE GREATNESS WHEN I BECOME KING OF FRANCE. HIS JOKE WON'T BE FUNNY WHEN WE GO TO WAR. HE WILL BE RESPONSIBLE FOR THE LOSS OF THOUSANDS OF LIVES.

ALL FRENCHMEN WILL *REGRET* THE DAUPHIN'S JOKE!

I ASK GOD TO HELP ME. IN HIS NAME I AM GOING TO FIGHT.

THE DAUPHIN'S JOKE WILL SEEM VERY BAD WHEN THOUSANDS SUFFER BECAUSE OF IT.

LET THEM GO.

GOODBYE.

THAT WASN'T A NICE MESSAGE.

THE DAUPHIN WILL BE SORRY THAT HE SENT IT!

GET READY TO GO TO FRANCE!

LET'S GET READY AS FAST AS WE CAN.

WE'LL TEACH THIS DAUPHIN A LESSON HE WON'T FORGET!

24

SOUTHAMPTON - SUMMER 1415.
THE SHIPS ARE PREPARING TO LEAVE FOR FRANCE.

THE KING IS TAKING A RISK BY TRUSTING THOSE THREE MEN.

HE WILL HAVE THEM *ARRESTED* SOON.

HOW COOL AND CALM THEY ARE!

THE KING KNOWS ABOUT THEIR PLANS.

HOW CAN THEY *BETRAY* THE KING LIKE THIS?

YOU KNOW HOW MUCH I GAVE THE *LORD* OF CAMBRIDGE. HE HAS PLANNED TO KILL ME FOR A FEW GOLD COINS.

I'VE GIVEN A LOT TO THIS MAN TOO, AND HE PLANS TO DO THE SAME.

AND WHAT CAN I SAY TO YOU, LORD SCROOP?

YOU WERE MY CLOSEST ADVISER, YOU KNEW ME WELL. HOW COULD YOU DO THIS TO ME?

THIS IS UNBELIEVABLE.

THE *DEVIL* WHO MADE YOU DO THIS IS THE WORST DEVIL OF ALL, BECAUSE YOU HAD NO REASON TO DO IT.

34

35

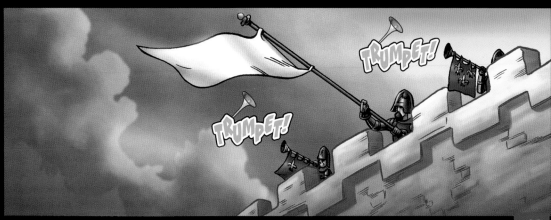

49

FRANCE – THE *PALACE* OF ROUEN – 20TH OCTOBER 1415
KING CHARLES VI IS ANGRY AT THE FRENCH DEFEAT AT HARFLEUR ...

HE'S *CROSSED* THE RIVER SOMME.

IF WE DON'T STOP HIM NOW, WE SHOULD JUST GO AND LEAVE EVERYTHING TO THEM.

IT'S THE *NORMANS'* *FAULT.* THEY WENT TO ENGLAND AND PRODUCED THESE PEOPLE WHO ARE NOW ATTACKING US.

IF WE DON'T STOP THEM, I'LL SELL MY LAND AND BUY A DIRTY PIG FARM IN BRITAIN!

WHERE DO THEY GET THEIR STRENGTH FROM? ISN'T ENGLAND FOGGY AND COLD? THE SUN RARELY SHINES AND ALL THEIR FRUIT DIES. CAN THE DIRTY WATER THAT THEY CALL *BEER* WARM THEIR COLD BLOOD?

STOP THE KING OF ENGLAND WHO IS **ADVANCING** THROUGH OUR LAND. HIS **FLAGS** ARE PAINTED IN THE BLOOD OF HARFLEUR. ATTACK HIM, DEFEAT HIM AND BRING HIM TO ROUEN.

NOW YOU'RE TALKING LIKE A KING. THE ENGLISH **ARMY** IS SMALL, AND THE SOLDIERS ARE SICK AND HUNGRY. I'M SURE WHEN HENRY SEES OUR ARMY HE'LL OFFER US MONEY TO LET HIM GO.

GO QUICKLY TO MONTJOY AND LET HIM ASK THE ENGLISH KING HOW MUCH HE WILL PAY US. **PRINCE DAUPHIN**, YOU'LL STAY HERE IN ROUEN.

NO! PLEASE LET ME GO!

BE **PATIENT.** STAY WITH ME.

THE REST OF YOU, GO, AND QUICKLY BRING ME NEWS OF HENRY'S **SURRENDER.**

57

FRANCE – THE ENGLISH CAMP OF PICARDY – 23RD OCTOBER 1415 NEAR THE BRIDGE OVER THE RIVER TERNOISE ...

HOW ARE YOU, *CAPTAIN* FLUELLEN? HAVE YOU COME FROM THE BRIDGE?

LET ME TELL YOU, THERE'S BEEN SOME HEAVY FIGHTING THERE.

IS THE *DUKE* OF EXETER SAFE?

HE IS SUCH A GREAT MAN. HE'S UNHURT AND HE'S DEFENDING THE BRIDGE VERY *BRAVELY.*

THERE WAS AN OLD SOLDIER AT THE BRIDGE WHO WAS VERY BRAVE.

WHAT WAS HIS NAME?

ANCIENT PISTOL.

I DON'T KNOW HIM.

HERE HE COMES.

CAPTAIN, CAN I ASK YOU A FAVOUR? THE *DUKE* OF EXETER THINKS VERY HIGHLY OF YOU ...

YES, HE DOES, AND I'VE EARNED HIS RESPECT.

THERE'S A *BRAVE* SOLDIER CALLED BARDOLPH WHO'S HAD SOME VERY BAD LUCK-

LUCK IS A BLIND THING, ANCIENT PISTOL, AND ALWAYS CHANGING.

IT ROLLS AND ROLLS AND ROLLS.

LUCK HAS NOT BEEN KIND TO BARDOLPH. HE STOLE SOMETHING FROM A CHURCH AND THEY'RE GOING TO *HANG* HIM FOR IT.

EXETER HAS SAID HE MUST DIE. PLEASE SPEAK TO THE DUKE ABOUT HIM. HE WILL LISTEN TO YOU. DON'T LET BARDOLPH DIE AT THE END OF A ROPE. ASK FOR HIS LIFE, AND I'LL REPAY YOU.

I THINK I UNDERSTAND WHAT YOU MEAN.

66

IMAGINE THAT IT'S DARK AND YOU CAN HEAR THE SOUNDS OF BOTH ARMIES IN THEIR CAMPS.

THE *GUARDS* IN ONE CAMP CAN ALMOST HEAR THE WHISPERS OF THE GUARDS IN THE OTHER CAMP AND THEY CAN SEE THE OTHERS' SHADOWY FACES IN THE LIGHT FROM THE CAMPFIRES.

THE HORSES THREATEN EACH OTHER AND MEN NOISILY PREPARE THEIR *MASTERS'* ARMOUR.

THE BIRDS BEGIN TO SING AND *BELLS* RING THE HOUR – IT'S THREE O'CLOCK.

73

78

BROTHER JOHN BATES, IS IT MORNING?

I THINK SO. BUT WE HAVE NO REASON TO WANT MORNING TO COME.

WE'RE WATCHING THE BEGINNING OF THE DAY, BUT I DON'T THINK WE'LL SEE THE END OF IT.

WHO GOES THERE?

A FRIEND.

WHO'S YOUR *CAPTAIN?*

SIR THOMAS ERPINGHAM.

A GOOD OFFICER AND A *GENTLEMAN.* WHAT DOES HE THINK OF OUR SITUATION?

HE THINKS WE'LL LOSE THE *BATTLE.*

HAS HE TOLD THE KING THAT?

HE GETS FRIGHTENED BY THE SAME THINGS AS US, AND SO NO ONE SHOULD APPEAR AFRAID IN FRONT OF HIM. THEY MIGHT MAKE THE KING AFRAID, WHO WOULD THEN MAKE THE *ARMY* WORRIED.

NO, AND HE SHOULDN'T.

THE KING'S JUST A MAN LIKE THE REST OF US. HE HAS THE SAME FEELINGS AS US.

81

83

89

91

95

98

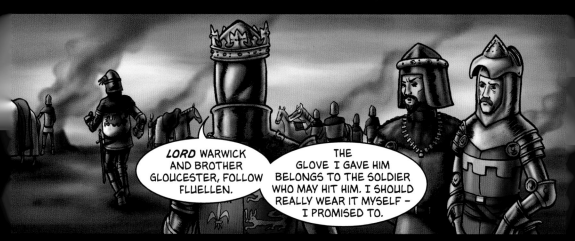

121

123

124

129

131

SO I HAVE TO WAIT UNTIL SUMMER TO CATCH HER. AND EVEN THEN, SHE MUST BE BLIND?

LIKE LOVE IS, MY *LORD*, BEFORE ITS EYES ARE OPENED.

THAT'S RIGHT.

I'M BLIND MYSELF. I CAN'T SEE ALL THE BEAUTIFUL FRENCH CITIES BECAUSE THERE'S ONE LOVELY FRENCH GIRL WHO STANDS IN MY WAY.

YES, MY LORD. YOU SEE ALL THE CITIES AS GIRLS.

WILL KATE BE MY WIFE?

IF THAT'S WHAT YOU WANT.

IF THE CITIES YOU'VE TALKED ABOUT COME WITH HER, I'LL BE HAPPY. THEN SHE'LL HELP ME GET WHAT I WANT.

WE'VE AGREED TO ALL REASONABLE DEMANDS.

IS THAT RIGHT, MY LORDS?

THE KING HAS AGREED TO THEM ALL – HIS DAUGHTER FIRST, AND THEN THE OTHERS.

THERE'S ONLY ONE THING HE HASN'T AGREED TO YET.

YOUR HIGHNESS WANTS HIM TO WRITE TO YOU AS 'OUR DEAR SON HENRY, KING OF ENGLAND AND THE NEXT KING OF FRANCE'.

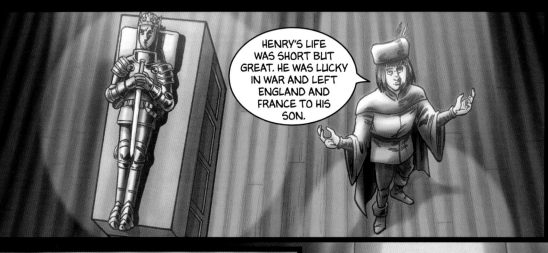

134

Henry V

End

Glossary

A

advance /æd'va:ns/ – (advances, advancing, advanced) To advance or to make an advance means to move forward, often in order to attack someone.

ambassador /æm'bæsədə/ – (ambassadors) An ambassador is an important official who lives in a foreign country and represents the government of his or her own country.

angel /'eɪndʒəl/ – (angels) Angels are spiritual beings that some people believe are God's messengers and servants in heaven. If you refer to someone as an angel, you mean that they are good, kind and gentle.

annoy /ə'nɔɪ/ – (annoys, annoying, annoyed) If someone annoys you, they make you quite angry and impatient.

archbishop /'a:tʃ'bɪʃəp/ – (archbishops) In the Roman Catholic church, and in some other churches, an archbishop is a bishop of the highest rank.

armour /'a:mə/ In former times, armour was the protective metal clothing worn by soldiers.

army /'a:mi/ – (armies) An army is a large organised group of people who are armed and trained to fight.

arrest /ə'rest/ – (arrests, arresting, arrested) When the police arrest someone or make an arrest, they take them to a police station in order to decide whether they should be charged with an offence.

B

bald /bɔ:ld/ – (balder, baldest) Someone who is bald has little or no hair on the top of their head.

battle /'bætəl/ – (battles) In a war, a battle is a fight between armies or between groups of ships or planes.

battlefield /'bætəlfi:ld/ – (battlefields) – A battlefield is a place where a battle is fought.

beer /bɪə/ – (beers) Beer is a bitter alcoholic drink made from grain. A beer is a glass of beer.

bell /bel/ – (bells) A bell is a device that makes a ringing sound which attracts people's attention. It can also be a hollow metal object with a loose piece hanging inside it that hits the sides and makes a sound.

betray /bɪ'treɪ/ – (betrays, betraying, betrayed) If someone betrays their country or their comrades, they give information to an enemy, putting their country's security or their comrades' safety at risk.

bishop /'bɪʃəp/ – (bishops) A bishop is a clergyman of high rank.

bleed /bli:d/ – (bleeds, bleeding, bled) When you bleed, you lose blood from your body as a result of injury or illness.

bless /bles/ – (blesses, blessing, blessed) When a priest blesses people or things, he or she asks for God's favour and protection for them.

blow on /bləʊ ɒn/ To blow on something, means to attack it.

brave /breɪv/ – (bravely, braver, bravest) Someone who is brave is willing to do dangerous things, and does not show fear in difficult or dangerous situations.

C

cannon /'kænən/ – (cannons) A cannon is a large gun on wheels, formerly used in battles.

captain /'kæptɪn/ – (captains) A captain is a military officer of middle rank.

ceremony /'serɪməni/ Ceremony consists of the special things that are said and done on very formal occasions.

chin /tʃɪn/ – (chins) Your chin is the part of your face below your mouth and above your neck.

cloak /kləʊk/ – (cloaks) A cloak is a wide loose coat that fastens at the neck and does not have sleeves.

confident /'kɒnfɪdənt/ If you are confident about something, you are certain that it will happen in the way you want it to.

conquer /'kɒŋkə/ – (conquers, conquering, conquered) If one country or group of people conquers another, they take complete control of their land.

consider /kən'sɪdə/ – (considers, considering, considered) If you consider something, you think about it carefully.

Cornish /'kɔ:rɪʃ/ When you describe a person or thing to be Cornish, it means that person or thing has something to do with Cornwall, England, its inhabitants, or the Cornish language.

corporal /'kɔ:prəl/ – (corporals) A corporal is a non-commissioned officer in the army.

cousin /'kʌzən/ – (cousins) Your cousin is the child of your uncle or aunt.

crime /kraɪm/ – (crimes) A crime is an illegal action or activity for which a person can be punished by law.

criticise /'krɪtɪsaɪz/ – (criticises, criticising, criticised) If you criticise someone or something, you express your disapproval of them by saying what you think is wrong with them.

cross /krɒs/ – (crosses, crossing, crossed) If you cross a room, road, or area of land, you move to the other side of it. If you cross to a place, you move over a room, road, or area in order to reach that place.

curly /'kɜːli/ – (curlier, curliest) Curly hair is full of curls.

D

Dauphin /'dɔːfɪn/ The title Dauphin was used from 1349 to 1830 to refer to the eldest son of the king of France.

destroy /dɪ'strɔɪ/ – (destroys, destroying, destroyed) To destroy something means to cause so much damage to it that it is completely ruined or does not exist any more.

devil /'devəl/ – (devils) A devil is an evil spirit.

dice /daɪs/ – A dice is a small cube with one to six spots on each face, used in games.

dishonest /dɪs'ɒnɪst/ If you say someone is dishonest, you mean that they are not honest and you cannot trust them.

disrespect /dɪsrə'spekt/ When you treat someone with disrespect, you treat them with rudeness or contempt.

drum /drʌm/ – (drums) A drum is a musical instrument consisting of a skin stretched tightly over a round frame.

duke /duːk/ – (dukes) A duke is a noble of high rank.

E

earl /əːl/ – (earls) An earl is a British nobleman ranking between a marquis and a viscount.

elbow /'elbeʊ/ – (elbows) Your elbow is the joint where your arm bends in the middle.

emperor /'empərə/ – (emperors) An emperor is a man who rules as an empire.

enemy /'enəmi/ – (enemies) Your enemy is someone who intends to harm you.

engaged /ɪn'geɪdʒd/ If two people are engaged, they have agreed to marry each other.

F

fame /feɪm/ If you achieve fame, you become very well known.

fault /fɔːlt/ If a bad situation is your fault, you caused it or are responsible for it.

flag /flæg/ – (flags) A flag is a piece of coloured cloth used as a sign for something or as a signal.

flat /flæt/ Something that is flat is level and smooth.

forbid /fə'bɪd/ – If you forbid someone to do something, or if you forbid an activity, you order that it must not be done.

G

gentleman /'dʒentəlmən/ – (gentlemen) A gentleman is a man who is polite and well educated.

glad /glæd/ If you are glad about something, you are happy and pleased about it.

glove /glʌv/ Gloves are pieces of clothing which cover your hand and wrist and have individual sections for each finger.

greeting /'griːtɪŋ/ A greeting is something friendly that you say or do when you meet someone.

guard /gaːd/ – (guards, guarding, guarded) If you guard a place, person, or object, you watch them carefully, either to protect them or to stop them from escaping. A guard is someone such as a soldier or prison officer who is protecting a particular place or person. When a soldier or prison officer is guarding someone or something, you say that they are on guard or standing guard.

H

hang /hæŋ/ – (hangs, hanging, hung) If someone is hanged, they are killed by having a rope tied around their neck and the support taken away from under their feet.

heaven /'hevən/ In some religions, heaven is said to be the place where God lives and where good people go when they die.

hell /hel/ According to some religions, hell is the place where the Devil lives, and where wicked people are sent to be punished when they die.

High Constable /haɪ 'kɒnstəbl/ The title High Constable is given to the person who is the chief of the force of policemen and officers of a district or city.

horseman /'hɔːsmən/ – (horsemen) A horseman is a man who is riding a horse, or who rides horses well.

holy /ˈhəʊli/ – (holier, holiest) Something that is holy is considered to be special because it relates to God or to a particular religion.

J

jealousy /ˈdʒeləsi/ – (jealousies) Jealousy is the feeling of anger or bitterness which someone has when they think that another person is trying to take a lover, friend, or possession away from them, or when they wish that they could have the qualities or possessions that another person has.

Judgement Day /dʒʌdʒmənt dei / Judgement Day is the day on which the Last Judgement is believed to take place. In some beliefs the Last Judgement is the judgement expected to take place at the end of the world.

K

kingdom /ˈkɪŋdəm/ – (kingdoms) A kingdom is a country or region that is ruled by a king or a queen.

L

leek /liːk/ – (leeks) Leeks are long green and white vegetables which smell similar to onions.

lieutenant /lefˈtenənt/ – (lieutenants) A lieutenant is a junior officer in the army, navy, or air force.

lip /lɪp/ – (lips) Your lips are the two outer parts of the edge of your mouth.

lodger /ˈlɒdʒə/ – (lodgers) A lodger is someone who pays rent to live in someone else's home.

lord /lɔːd/ – (lords) In Britain, a lord is a man who has a high rank in the nobility. *Lord* is a title used in front of the names of some male members of the nobility, and of judges, bishops, and some high ranking officials.

low-born /ləʊbɔːn/ A person who is low-born is someone born to a family of low social status.

M

mend /mend/ – (mends, mending, mended) If you mend something that is damaged or broken, you repair it so that it works properly or can be used.

messenger /ˈmesɪndʒə/ – (messengers) A messenger takes a message to someone, or takes messages regularly as their job.

mistaken /mɪˈsteɪkən/ If you are mistaken, or if you have a mistaken belief, you are wrong about something.

monster /ˈmɒnstə/ – (monsters) A monster is a large imaginary creature that is very frightening.

N

nail /neɪl/ – (nails) Your nails are the thin hard parts that grow at the ends of your fingers and toes.

neck /nek/ – (necks) Your neck is the part of your body which joins your head to the rest of your body.

the Normans /ˈnɔːməns/ Normandy, France. A Norman also refers to a descendant of the people of mixed Scandinavian and Frankish origin established there in the 10th century, who conquered England in 1066.

O

obey /əʊˈbeɪ/ – (obeys, obeying, obeyed) If you obey a rule, instruction, or person, you do what you are told to do.

P

pardon /ˈpaːdən/ – (pardons, pardoning, pardoned) You say 'Pardon?', or 'I beg your pardon?' or, in American English, 'Pardon me?' when you want someone to repeat what they have just said, either because you have not heard or understood it or because you are surprised by it. If someone who has been found guilty of a crime is pardoned or is given a pardon, they are officially allowed to go free and are not punished.

pass (a law) /paːs/ When people in authority pass a new law or a proposal, they formally agree to it or approve it.

pillow /ˈpɪləʊ/ – (pillows) A pillow is a rectangular cushion which you rest your head on when you are in bed.

pistol /ˈpɪstəl/ – (pistols) A pistol is a small handgun.

pity /ˈpɪti/ If you feel pity for someone, you feel very sorry for them.

prince /prɪns/ – A prince is a male member of a royal family, especially the son of a king or queen.

princess /ˌprɪnˈses/ – (princesses) A princess is a female member of a royal family, especially the daughter of a king or queen or the wife of a prince.

prove /pruːv/ – (proves, proving, proved or proven) If you prove something, you show by means of argument or evidence that it is definitely true.

R

regret /rɪˈgret/ – (regrets, regretting, regretted) If you regret something that you have done, you wish that you had not done it.

respected /rɪˈspektɪd/ Someone or something that is respected is admired and considered important by many people.

Roman /ˈrəʊmən/ – (Romans) Roman means related to or connected with ancient Rome and its empire. A Roman was a citizen of ancient Rome or its empire.

S

saint /seɪnt/ – (saints) A saint is a dead person who is officially recognised and honoured by the Christian church because his or her life was a perfect example of the way Christians should live.

the Scots /skɒts/ A Scot is a person who is a native or inhabitant of Scotland.

shake off /ʃeɪk ɒf/ If you shake off someone or something that you do not want, you manage to get away from them or get rid of them.

shame /ʃeɪm/ Shame is an uncomfortable feeling that you have when you know that you have done something wrong or embarrassing, or when someone close to you has.

shield /ʃiːld/ – (shields) A shield is a large piece of metal or leather which soldiers used to carry to protect their bodies while they were fighting.

spear /spɪə/ – (spears) A spear is a weapon consisting of a long pole with a sharp point.

square /skweə/ – (squares) A square is a shape with four sides of the same length and four corners that are all right angles.

surrender /səˈrendə/ – (surrenders, surrendering, surrendered) If you surrender, you stop fighting or resisting someone or something and agree that you have been beaten. Surrender is the act of surrendering.

sword /sɔːd/ – (swords) A sword is a weapon with a handle and a long blade.

T

the Thames /teɪmz/ The Thames is the longest river in England which flows eastward through London to the North Sea.

throne /θrəʊn/ – (thrones) A throne is an ornate chair used by a king, queen or emperor on important occasions. You can talk about the throne as a way of referring to the position of being king, queen or emperor.

tragic /ˈtrædʒɪk/ Something that is tragic is extremely sad, usually because it involves death or suffering.

traitor /ˈtreɪtə/ – (traitors) A traitor is someone who betrays their country or a group of which they are a member by helping their enemies.

trick /trɪk/ – (tricks, tricking, tricked) If someone tricks you, or if they play a trick on you, they deceive you, often in order to make you do something.

W

wave /weɪv/ – (waves) A wave is a raised mass of water on the sea or a lake, caused by the wind or the tide.

wedding /ˈwedɪŋ/ A wedding is a marriage ceremony and the celebration that often takes place afterwards.

wine /waɪn/ – (wines) Wine is an alcoholic drink, usually made from grapes.

wisely /ˈwaɪzli/ If you have done something wisely, you have used your experience and knowledge to make sensible decisions and judgements.

Y

Your Highness /jɔːˈhaɪnɪs/ You use expressions such as Your Highness and His Highness to address or refer to a member of a royal family.

William Shakespeare

(c.1564 - 1616 AD)

Many people believe that William Shakespeare was the greatest writer in the English language. He wrote 38 plays, 154 sonnets, and five poems. His plays have been translated into every major living language.

The actual date of Shakespeare's birth is unknown. Most people accept that his birthday was 23rd April 1564. He died on the same date, 52 years later.

The life of William Shakespeare can be divided into three acts. He lived in the small village of Stratford-upon-Avon until he was 20 years old. There, he studied, got married and had children. Then Shakespeare lived as an actor and playwright (writer of plays) in London. Finally, when he was about 50, Shakespeare retired back to his hometown. He enjoyed some wealth gained from his successful years of work — but died a few years later.

William Shakespeare was the eldest son of tradesman John Shakespeare and Mary Arden. He was the third of eight children. William Shakespeare was lucky to survive childhood. Sixteenth century England was filled with diseases such as smallpox, tuberculosis, typhus and dysentery. The average length of life was 35 years. Three of Shakespeare's seven siblings died from what was probably the Bubonic Plague.

Few records exist about Shakespeare's life. According to most accounts, he went to the local grammar school and studied English literature and Latin. When he was 18 years old, he married Anne Hathaway. She was a local farmer's daughter. They had three children: Susanna in 1583, and twins Hamnet and Judith in 1585. Hamnet, Shakespeare's only son, died when he was 11.

Shakespeare moved to London in 1587. He was an actor at The Globe Theatre. This was one of the largest theatres in England. He appeared in public as a poet in 1593. Later on, in 1599, he became part-owner of The Globe.

When Queen Elizabeth died in 1603, her cousin James became King. He supported Shakespeare and his actors. He allowed them to be called the 'King's Men' as long as they entertained the court.

Between 1590 and 1613, Shakespeare wrote his plays, sonnets and poems. The first plays are thought to have been comedies and histories. He was to become famous for both types of writing. Next, he mainly wrote tragedies until about 1608. These included *Hamlet, King Lear* and *Macbeth,* which are considered three of the best examples of writing in the English language. In his last phase, Shakespeare wrote tragicomedies, also known as romances. His final play was *Henry VII,* written two years before his death.

Shakespeare's cause of death is unknown. He was buried at the Church of the Holy Trinity in Stratford-upon-Avon. His gravestone has the words (believed to have been written by Shakespeare himself) on it:

Good friend for Jesus sake forbear,
To dig the dust enclosed here!
Blessed be the man that spares these stones,
And cursed be he that moves my bones.

In his will, Shakespeare left most of his possessions to his eldest daughter, Susanna. He left his wife, Anne, his 'second best bed' — but nobody knows what this gift meant. Shakespeare's last direct descendant, his granddaughter, died in 1670.

Henry V, King of England

(c.1387 - 1422 AD)

Henry V was a great warrior king in medieval England. He is famous mostly because he won the Battle of Agincourt.

Henry V was born in 1387. He was the oldest son of Henry IV and Mary Bohun. His mother died when Henry was ten. When his father became King in 1399, Henry became the Prince of Wales. His other titles were Duke of Lancaster and Duke of Cornwall.

Henry trained as a solider. By the time he was 16 years old, Henry had fought in several important battles. He was also interested in government, which caused him to argue a lot with his father. When he was 26 years old, Henry became King of England.

As soon as he became King, Henry V wanted to rule England as a unified nation. Past arguments were to be forgotten. However, two years later, Edmund Mortimer, the Earl of March, tried to become King. Henry managed to stop Mortimer. His position as ruler was made stronger as a result. He did not have any more problems in England while he was King.

In 1415, Henry sailed to France. For the rest of his rule, his attention was focused on the French. Henry wanted to become the King of France. To do this, he had to gain back some land for the English. This land was the focus of the French war.

First, Henry won the port of Harfleur. Then, on 25th October 1415, he defeated the French at the Battle of Agincourt. Between 1417 and 1419, Henry continued to succeed. He conquered Normandy and Picardy. He forced the French to agree to the Treaty of Troyes in May 1420.

National Portrait Gallery, London

The Treaty of Troyes recognised Henry as heir and regent of France. When Charles VI, the current King of France died, Henry would be crowned King. In June, 1420, Henry married Katherine of Valois, daughter of the King of France. The marriage was designed to bring peace to the two countries.

Henry and Katherine returned to England for a short trip. One year after his wedding, he sailed back to France for what would be his final battle. In August 1422, Henry V died suddenly. His death was probably caused by dysentery, which is an infection of the gut. He was 34 years old. He did not live long enough to be crowned King of France, as Charles VI didn't die until two months later. Henry V was buried in Westminster Abbey.

Henry V was succeeded by his nine-month-old son, Henry VI. This child was crowned King of England in 1429. Due to his father's efforts, Henry VI became King of France in 1431.

Notes

Notes

Audio Track Listing

Henry V

CD 1

Track 1	Copyright notice
Track 2	Act 1 Prologue
Track 3	Act 1 Scene 1
Track 4	Act 1 Scene 2
Track 5	Act 2 Prologue
Track 6	Act 2 Scene 1
Track 7	Act 2 Scene 2
Track 8	Act 2 Scene 3
Track 9	Act 2 Scene 4
Track 10	Act 3 Prologue
Track 11	Act 3 Scene 1
Track 12	Act 3 Scene 2
Track 13	Act 3 Scene 3
Track 14	Act 3 Scene 4
Track 15	Act 3 Scene 5
Track 16	Act 3 Scene 6
Track 17	Act 3 Scene 7

CD 2

Track 1	Copyright notice
Track 2	Act 4 Prologue
Track 3	Act 4 Scene 1
Track 4	Act 4 Scene 2
Track 5	Act 4 Scene 3
Track 6	Act 4 Scene 4
Track 7	Act 4 Scene 5
Track 8	Act 4 Scene 6
Track 9	Act 4 Scene 7
Track 10	Act 4 Scene 8
Track 11	Act 5 Prologue
Track 12	Act 5 Scene 1
Track 13	Act 5 Scene 2
Track 14	Epilogue

OTHER CLASSICAL COMICS TITLES:

Macbeth	Great Expectations	Frankenstein

Available now	Available now	Available now